100

Writing

Prompts

Creative Writing Books

In the 100 writing prompts journal, you have over 100 random titles and 2 pages to fill with whatever you can concoct. Challenge yourself to fill all the pages and spark your imagination. Some titles will bring out the best in you, whereas others may become your greatest obstacle to date. The point is to practice your writing skills and improve with every passing day.

Here are few suggestions to make the most of this writing prompt journal:
• Time each writing session
• Never skip a title even if you can't think of anything immediately
• Limit your story to two pages
• Expand your best stories into full-length novels or even add them to a collection of short stories
• Fill the entire notebook, then type out each story to refine your editing and proofreading skills
• Share your stories with friends & family

There are no limitations to what you can do in this unique writing prompt journal, so don't hold back and have fun!

-Creative Writing Books

NOTES

Lonely Hospital Pirates

Lonely Hospital Pirates

The Whispering Wave

The Whispering Wave

The Energetic Nurse's Happiness

The Energetic Nurse's Happiness

Body In The Courage

Body In The Courage

The Corporate Greed's Visions

The Corporate Greed's Visions

Son In The Wife

Son In The Wife

The Light Of The Happiness

The Light Of The Happiness

Sleeping West Holster

Sleeping West Holster

The Only Medicine

The Only Medicine

Child In The Twilight

Child In The Twilight

Frame In The Dozen

Frame In The Dozen

The Twilight Of The Happiness

The Twilight Of The Happiness

Last West Settlers

Last West Settlers

The Emerald Sons

The Emerald Sons

Spaniard In The Window

Spaniard In The Window

The Loneliness's Promise

The Loneliness's Promise

Children In The Gentleman

Children In The Gentleman

The Leather Of The Cowboy

The Leather Of The Cowboy

First Writer Feeding

First Writer Feeding

The Modern Day

The Modern Day

Aftermath In The Shadowmarch

Aftermath In The Shadowmarch

The Tornado's Wizard

The Tornado's Wizard

Wolf In The Vampire

Wolf In The Vampire

The Prey Of The Writer

The Prey Of The Writer

Tentative California Laird

Tentative California Laird

The Luscious Lass

The Luscious Lass

The Loyal California's Murderer

The Loyal California's Murderer

Queen In The Stallion

Queen In The Stallion

The Murderer's Starlight

The Murderer's Starlight

Ship In The Winter

Ship In The Winter

The Portal Of The Murderer

The Portal Of The Murderer

Day Of The Astronaut Abyss

Day Of The Astronaut Abyss

The Clash Of The Punch

The Clash Of The Punch

Uranus In The Frequency

Uranus In The Frequency

The Truthfulness's Monster

The Truthfulness's Monster

Tribulation In The Prince

Tribulation In The Prince

The Terran Of The Astronaut

The Terran Of The Astronaut

The Chronicles Of The Blue

The Chronicles Of The Blue

Oblivion In The Half-Life

Oblivion In The Half-Life

The Lost's Solar

The Lost's Solar

The Empire Of The Lost

The Empire Of The Lost

Shadowy Canada Petals

Shadowy Canada Petals

The Eager Winter

The Eager Winter

Year In The Waves

Year In The Waves

Ashes In The End

Ashes In The End

The Wild Vision

The Wild Vision

The Thief Veterinarian's Friendship

The Thief Veterinarian's Friendship

Boy In The Flames

Boy In The Flames

Word In The Lords

Word In The Lords

Lone Deserted Island Snake

Lone Deserted Island Snake

The Sweet Lover

The Sweet Lover

The Inspirational Manager's Corruption

The Inspirational Manager's Corruption

Bible In The Savior

Bible In The Savior

The Corruption's Dreamer

The Corruption's Dreamer

Echo In The Wizards

Echo In The Wizards

Charnel Castle Ring

Charnel Castle Ring

The Light Rule

The Light Rule

Codex In The Journal

Codex In The Journal

Sea In The Wall

Sea In The Wall

The Choice Of The Friendship

The Choice Of The Friendship

Destroy Airplane Theorem

Destroy Airplane Theorem

The Underworld Giant

The Underworld Giant

Warp In The Half-Life

Warp In The Half-Life

The Boss's Lord

The Boss's Lord

Cube In The Bug

Cube In The Bug

The Angel Of The Officer

The Angel Of The Officer

Some Bahamas Velvet

Some Bahamas Velvet

The Flaming Moonlight

The Flaming Moonlight

The Stubborn Wedding Planner's Ex-Husband

The Stubborn Wedding Planner's Ex-Husband

Lad & The Sorcerer

Lad & The Sorcerer

Dove In The Nightingale

Dove In The Nightingale

Dwindling San Francisco Thief

Dwindling San Francisco Thief

The Weeping Healer

The Weeping Healer

The Bold Cop's Retirement

The Bold Cop's Retirement

Dream In The Silence

Dream In The Silence

The Disease's Birth

The Disease's Birth

Hustler In The Hunter

Hustler In The Hunter

Green Pimp Luck

Green Pimp Luck

The Wanton Person

The Wanton Person

The Independent New York's Rivals

The Independent New York's Rivals

Nothing In The River

Nothing In The River

Guardian In The Waves

Guardian In The Waves

Fellowship Of The Orlando Labyrinth

Fellowship Of The Orlando Labyrinth

The Wolf Queen

The Wolf Queen

Fairy In The Nature

Fairy In The Nature

The Haunted Texas Sire

The Haunted Texas Sire

The Mortal Three

The Mortal Three

The Man Of The World

The Man Of The World

Every Gambler's Eye

Every Gambler's Eye

The Dangerous Weeping

The Dangerous Weeping

The Ice Of The Poor

The Ice Of The Poor

The Wild Male

The Wild Male

Past In The Flowers

Past In The Flowers

Slithering Runner Mage

Slithering Runner Mage

The Final Waves

The Final Waves

Prized Mexico Game

Prized Mexico Game

The Frozen Slaves

The Frozen Slaves

The Silk Of The Phoenix

The Silk Of The Phoenix

Forgotten Dude Woman

Forgotten Dude Woman

Absent Space Witches

Absent Space Witches